The Freudian Fallacy

Also available by the same author:

1. »Wenn Glaube krank macht. Das Sacco Syndrom«
   BoD – Books on Demand
   ISBN 978-3-7392-7310-5

2. »Die Neurose Sigmund Freuds als Kollektivneurose«
   BoD – Books on Demand
   ISBN 978-3-7392-7544-4

3. »Homosexualität, Heterosexualität, Pädophilie«
   BoD – Books on Demand
   ISBN 978-3-7392-8606-8

4. »Ursachen des Masochismus. Analyse des Masochismus am Beispiel der Straßenprostitution, des Borderline-Syndroms und der ›endogenen Depression‹«
   BoD – Books on Demand
   ISBN 978-3-7392-8607-5

FRANK SACCO

Author of „Sacco-Syndrome"

The Freudian Fallacy

Neurosis inherent in Psychoanalysis

Bibliographical Information of the Deutsche Nationalbibliothek

This publication is listed in the Deutsche Nationalbibliographie of the Deutsche Nationalbibliothek; detailed bibliographical information can be accessed under http: //dnb.d-nb.de

© 2016 Frank Sacco
Printing, Production and Layout: BoD – Books on Demand, Norderstedt
ISBN: 978-3-7392-6870-5

Contents

Preface	7
Freud's theory of fear	10
A modern look to the story of Oedipus	13
A modern look to the story of Prometheus	16
The biggest fear of girls	17
What about killing "your" God	18
Fear of God, fear of hell	20
Fear of circumcision (Jewish children)	21
Sexuality – a sin?	23
Save us from the fire of hell	25
The safest sex is no sex	26
A bad year: 2010	27
Jesus is free of sins	28
Back in the Middle Ages	30
Fear of God instead of fear of parents	32

Autism and the biggest fear	34
One is allowed to ask children	35
Psychiatrists and their fear of God	37
Criticism of psychiatrists	40
Delinquency, violence and the fear of hell	41
Guilty for an actual death by torture?	44
What our children need is a new religion	48
Freud killed his God Jahwe	50
A classic translation of Freud's neurosis	53
The EAT	57
A religious reform	58
" …we send to see … a theologian"	60
"Possessed by the devil"	61
What shall we do?	62
The poem	65

Preface

A change of paradigm in the field of psychiatry is due. The fear of castration is not, as Sigmund Freud mistakenly thought, the greatest of humanity's fears. With his various faints the supposed atheist Freud shows us the way to what is actually the greatest human fear, which was also his own: The fear of God.

This normally deeply suppressed fear of eternal punishment in the hereafter literally pulled the ground from under his feet. Indeed it led him to his addiction to nicotine, which finally brought about his death.

He led psychiatry – also through his misinterpretation of the Oedipus legend – into a diagnostic and therapeutic blind alley – a situation, which has now existed for over 100 years.

Only the psychoanalysis of the "atheist" Freud, which I present here, makes possible a new beginning in the field of psychiatry.

Churches increasingly radicalize. Pope Benedict launches crash courses in "exorcism" worldwide. A single Vatican priest, Father Gabriele Amorth, expelled 70,000 devils so far. The belief in devil and hell "comes out of every crack," it says in the newspaper "Die Zeit".

Since Luther we know that there is no devil: Luther's inkwell did not hit the devil, it landed on the wall instead. So Luther either was hallucinating or he was really bad in throwing.

The God of the Bible is simply unbearable, the doctor and psychoanalyst Tilman Moser recently commented accurately. In his writings he tries to – especially with regard to children – represent a "tolerable God". This is of course not possible with the Bible which in "blasphemy" attributes "acts of violence" to our God that are truly without equal as former Bishop Dr. M. Käßmann puts it within a different context. God had organized the Flood-Holocaust and the horrors of Sodom and Gomorrah and yet today he would manage a hell where he tortures diligently. During the Jubilee in 2000 the Vatican certified as "truth" that one could die just "at the mere sight" of torture if no one prevented death (in text).

This debases our God who indeed is love as we know as enlightened people. The Bible and our bible-related religion are supposed to frighten children. That this fear makes our children sick, because they are threatened with torture, the churches do know. But they don't care even though they know that the threat of torture means torture already and is strictly prohibited in the Federal Republic under Article 1 of the Grundgesetz – even for "gods". Our law does not provide exemptions for gods. "Obscene" calls philosopher Sloavoj Zizek the theological justification for the Holocaust in his book "Violence" if one claims that "all of these events had a deeper meaning". The only permissible reference to a Holocaust "should be a negative one." This also applies to the Flood. About such a final solution, we know that since 1945, there is nothing that you could celebrate. A prosecutor, however, judged it differently: It was "socially adequate" and the assessment of a Holocaust a just matter. I think on the contrary that it is antisocial, criminalizing, and – after the legislation – banned in Germany.

Let us turn now to truth and reason. At the beginning of every great truth there is always a blasphemy, so to read in the newspaper "Die Zeit", Oct. 13th 2011, p. 37. But in fact it is more special: At the be-ginning of a great truth there often is revealed a blasphemy of our churches. No god has ever burned alive an innocent Jewish child, therefore no God would ever have initiated Sodom. Torture and its "legitimacy" are works of man, they are never God's works. This sentence my sister was saying decades ago when she was studying theology. It always gives me a chill at the word blasphemy, since the churches have invented the term in order to burn red-haired women together with their red-haired children – alive, of course.

Let's look together at ways in which patients of health insurances are harmed by churches and in what way our psychiatry and basically a large part of our society can let this happen; how the insurances can get more mentally healthy members and how to save valuable money. Approximately more than 50% of psychiatric clients are patients suffering from anxiety- and guilt-diseases caused by the churches. They all might be entitled to an apology and financial compensation. Tournier considers their number for even greater. For more details please refer to the text. "Those who drink from the Bible without a filter system get insane," wrote George Bernard Shaw, and Gerhard Hauptmann also knew it. Our two major German churches, and it's all about them, have consistently ensured that it was never allowed to enter this filter system. A religion should be good for children. If it does the exact opposite and emotionally abuses children, it is not a religion. Then it is a Dysreligion.

Guilt is such a big word and usually it is too big. Psychiatrists are not necessarily to blame for what they do. The prejudice that exists in the population, psychiatrists themselves would be mentally ill, is not just a prejudice. They commit suicide four times more often than we internists and are thus four times more likely to suffer from depression. 40% of them are estimated to be substance-related addicts and about 17% had at least once been hospitalized for mental health reasons (Source: "Hilflose Helfer"). So these people really need help urgently – my help and the help of health insurances.

Freud's theory of fear

Until this day, psychoanalysis is based on Freud's theory that fear is a result of **a.) accumulated, unvented sexual tension, i.e. a direct translation of denied sexual desire or**

b.) the signal of a situation perceived as potentially dangerous and potentially causing trauma. Danger signals can be hidden behind in an unconscious intra-mental conflict.

Ref. a.)

I am not the only one who feels that it is pure theory to claim that sexuality is at the root of all fear. After all, one can have sex by oneself if the visit to the club was fruitless. Freud: "One may assume that the ego (in the case of unfulfilled arousal) senses dangers to which it reacts with fear." What kind of dangers are these supposed be that result from a lack of opportunity to experience sex? Surely one day the opportunity will offer itself. Here, patience is better than fear.

Ref. b.)

With all boys, the Oedipus complex plays a pivotal role in the genesis of the disease. At the bottom of it lies an archaic Greek myth of a brutal kind that, in general, a son will fall in love with his mother. He is jealous of his father and wants to get rid of him – and vice versa, the father the son. Finally, the son would want to kill the father. A small child (and later on the inner child in the unconscious mind of an adult), might now see himself in danger of suffering the consequences of his father's desire to castrate him, motivated by anger, revenge and jealousy, as the father also considers the son a rival for sexual love with the mother. We have all heard of this "fear of castration". For a start, this is inaccurate from a urological point of view. A castration is the removal of the testicles and not of the penis. However, let us not be pedantic, let us take a look at Freud's original publication, his "outline of psychoanalysis":

The mother wants to stop her male toddler from masturbating – to begin with unsuccessfully. "One day", the mother "remembers" that it is "not right …" that the son is sexually aroused. Finally, she will take the most effective measure and by telling her child that she "will tell the father and he will cut the penis off", says Freud. This fear of castration is "the most powerful trauma of his young life."

According to Freud, the age-old custom of circumcision is a "symbolic replacement of castration" and "an expression of submission to the father's authority". According to Freud, however, any girl's biggest trauma is the missing organ, thus leading to a feeling of inferiority, entirely pervading her identity. Freud cannot and may not acknowledge that the religious threat of being tormented in hell traumatizes a child far more gravely. At this point, he is completely inhibited by his neurosis which actually cuts the ground from under his feet in repeated fainting spells. Helpless, he is at the mercy of his God Jahwe, whom he was able to conquer in only 2% of his consciousness, not however in the 98% of his unconsciousness unaware to him. I always like to stress that a person is in fact unaware of his/her unconscious mind. This must be taken into account when someone is adamant that he/she does not believe in hell. What we actually do believe, we generally don't know, as we are not conscious of it.

Freud's theory (he himself is after all of Jewish ancestry) seems odd to Christians. But let's move on: How can a Jewish boy be afraid of his father doing such a terrible thing? Maybe circumcision used to mean significantly more and has survived purely as a "harmless" ritual. Perhaps it used to mean that cutting, the organ was cut off. That would have secured the chieftain exclusive access to his harem, as opposed to castration, where the ability to have sexual intercourse is retained. And as we know, in this respect, human beings are indeed equally inventive and brutal. I need only name the surgical sealing of the female vagina in African countries. This surgical intervention by the way is done by women exclusively, with zeal and using a razor blade. The seal is not opened again until the wedding night, by the husband. Eckhart Wisenhütter: "Circumcision is the symbolic replacement of castration which the forefather once imposed due to his own abundant absolute power." In "Religion and Depth Psychology".

A Christian child will hardly have a spontaneous fear of intervention in the genital area. It has not yet experienced such raw intervention, and most certainly not without anaesthetic. A Jewish boy in comparison usually experiences it frequently, first-hand and witnessing it happening to brothers and acquaintances. While for nearly all adults it is a "celebration", the injured child screams incessantly with pain.

To a Christian child the term "castration" will probably not mean a thing and it will therefore not suffer from any fears of that nature. My parents never threatened me with it, but my teacher in my first year of primary school used to frighten us regularly with eternal hell. That was where we would go if we lied too much. In a letter to Karl Abraham on May 3rd, 1908, Freud comments on "racial differences" in religion. In Germany after 1945 it is better to say: Indeed there are differences between "groups of people". According to more recent findings, which have, however, not gained general acceptance, the right to commit genocide must never be deduced from these minor differences. To deny differences in denial of reality is however no practicable way to go either.

A modern look to the story of Oedipus

The story of Oedipus can obviously also be seen differently, especially assuming that Freud simply shifted his religious conflicts to the sexual level. With Freud, the word hell hardly appears, because he was afraid of it. It never occurred to himself or probably to any psychiatrist that and why Freud feared God. Tensions resulting from sexual issues …. were much easier for him to bear than those caused by the mire of religion. The strongest human drive is related neither to sex nor death or aggression but to the avoidance of suffering. If we can avoid torment, we even immediately renounce sexual acts. A human being is essentially a uniquely timid creature. No other being but he understands that he can suffer permanent torture during his lifetime or even an – as the Church will claim up to this day – everlasting agony of punishment by torture. That is the only reason why the human being appears to be so evil – more evil than any animal. It is fear which makes him so cruel.

Here is my interpretation of the legend of Oedipus: Oedipus killed his father (without recognizing him as such) in a dispute after a traffic accident – perhaps even in selfdefence. That is all not so terribly bad. Far more profound was the act of incest he committed with Iokaste. As it turned out later, she was his mother. In "King Oedipus", Sophokles tries yet to comfort him: "Do not worry about your marriage to your mother"! However, incest is basically – as is patricide – not a problem related to sexology but it is a religious taboo, and one of the most major ones at that! That was worrying, that created feelings of guilt, that is what drove Oedipus to religious masochism: He burnt out both of his eyes. In order to not have to go to God's eternal torture chambers, he wanted to suffer here on earth. One offers one's God self-punishment to substitute agony in hell hoping that God will be satisfied with this sacrifice.

Today one lets the burning alone, today one becomes endogenously depressed and doesn't know why. The endogenously depressed person sacrifices his mental health to God. He wants to suffer, is however oblivious of this correlation. This means that Oedipus suffered from religious neurosis, the Sacco-Syndrome. He did not suffer from a parental problem but from a problem with God, with Hell. As a child, they had talked him and his wife into believing that religious incest was a religious taboo. Iokaste even hanged herself, a suicide induced by religion. The number of such suicides, for which our Churches are responsible, remains unchanged until this day. "A taboo takes revenge on itself", said Freud, and he erred. The breaker of a taboo only automatically and without being aware of it becomes a masochist unto his body or his soul, and that only if he knows of his breaking of the taboo. Before they had become aware of it, Oedipus and Iokaste had been happy. In the legend of Oedipus, the word hell does not occur.

The poet repressed it, just as adults do in our society. And yet, it is taught us for 15 years of our adolescence, and in this way it becomes a religious certainy. That is the professed goal of our Churches, and of course they reach this goal. 15 years of brainwashing naturally have an effect, and first of all, we cannot understand why modern psychiatry does not wish to see such a repercussion. It does is oblivious of fear of hell and does not permit it as diagnosis. Specialised training apparently on the subject does not exist and doctors who deal with the question are declared "paranoid psychotic". So what is wrong with this psychiatry? More about that later.

My God, by the way, who is Love, views incest in a more relaxed manner. After all, no great harm is done. Quite the opposite: Four healthy and, to start with, happy children of Oedipus materialize: Polyneikis, Eteokles, Ismene and even Antigone. It is only a crazy belief which makes them three-quarters orphans with a dead mother and a blind father. God is more likely to frown upon the priestly paedophile abuse which now shocks the world. He does not like that at all. Neither do any of us. Incest still counts as a deadly sin with the Catholics and is still severely punished according to § 173 of the Criminal Code– even if of the anti-baby-pill is used. Yet no lawyer understands why. It is said that the reason why incest is penalized is controversial.

It seems, however, that, according to our lawyers, incest represents a deeply rooted social taboo. Here, our religion is cheating its way into what should be a sensible science. I herewith wish to submit the notion to our judicial system to permit spontaneous, voluntary love affairs between adults, on condition that they initially use contraception or take counselling on the issue of human genetics. In his story "Sibling Love", the keen observer Goethe describes the damages caused by the Church in this field as a result of its prohibitions and their violation: suicide, depression, infant death and of course insanity.

A modern look to the story of Prometheus

Philosophers, sociologists and psychologists find it interpreting the myth of Prometheus difficult. Prometheus was a great sinner, his sin being helping us human beings to keep nice and warm. Gods often do not like that at all. They like to wear the trousers and want us to be cold. Therefore, Zeus chained the poor chap to a rock and an eagle had to tear out a piece of his liver every day – for centuries.

Present interpretations claim that there is no God as crazy as that, it is not possible that such a God exists. Moreover, we Christians supposedly know exactly that there is only the one God, namely ours. Therefore, Zeus was a fiction of the clerics, and a fiction cannot commission torture. Committing such a deadly sin, however, may have caused Prometheus, or, respectively, the later emulator of such "sins", to fall mortally ill, so ill that the patient and his/her environment simply had to accept divine punishment. In reality, it was self-punishment, a sacrifice I recognize today in ecclesiogenous depression. The Sacco-Syndrome, illnesses resulting from pathogenic religion, can also casually be called Prometheus or Oedipus Syndrome.

The biggest fear of girls

I decidedly doubt that "penis envy", according to Freud the female counterpart of fear of castration, exists with girls, causing consecutive feelings of inferiority, and even being responsible for making girls emotionally ill on a massive scale. Here, something is construed, and it always makes my female patients **laugh**. A penis of one's own may be important, it is, however, **not the center of this world** – also and in particular as far as women are concerned. If I were a girl, I would certainly not want a penis of my own, and if I had one growing, I would ask Daddy to actually have it cut off or at least shortened by a specialist, obviously under anaesthetic. I would not feel penis envy, on the contrary, I would insist on keeping my vagina and would like to be visited there by an attractive specimen.

Admittedly, it is by all means indisputably conceivable that girls may desire incest who would like to have father's "pride and joy" there. And they might get a God-Ego-Problem. That kind of thing is possibly just about conceivable for an internist. Freud does not realize that neither envy nor feelings of inferiority are feelings of fear and can therefore not counterpart them. From a urological point of view, it would be correct to counterpart fear of castration with a girl's fear of both ovaries being removed, amputation of the clitoris would counterpart fear of the penis being removed. Freud implored C. G. Jung to make a dogma of the sexual theory, saying it was absolutely the most essential. "You see, we must make it into a dogma, an unshakable bulwark …against the black mud slide of occultism".

What about killing "your" God

It must be said that Freud – quite rightly – put our two great religions (to which this paper solely refers) on a par with occultism. In this context, Jung says: "Evidently, he wanted to recruit me to join him in his **defence against threatening subconscious (religious, philosophical, the editor) contents**". In other words: Jung had a presentiment regarding Freud's actual fear. He was much less timid in his job and even spoke to schizophrenics about the bible. However, he had to do this secretly. Otherwise his Swiss colleagues would have declared him insane, Jung said. Freud however **needed a dogma as bulwark** against his actual fear, the fear of Jahwe's Hell: He had, after all, killed his God with the words "religion is insanity", and unfortunately, Gods do not like that at all. In doing so, Freud had committed the greatest sin possible for a Jew to commit. Our "Gods" live on in the subconscious and threaten the Ego with eternal revenge. Freud only received from them a neurosis due to fear of Hell. Only a few days after his "Antichrist" was published, Nietzsche, the "murderer of God" ("we murderers of all murderers), however, was "sent" many years of a schizophrenia due to fear of hell. As far as Nietzsche's disease is concerned, one must have thoughtlessly presumed, before the causative agent was discovered, that it might be a consequence of having syphilis. Whoever knows Nietzsche though, knows that he never had many intimate relationships with women. It is said that it was not until 1880 that the symptoms of syphilis-induced paralysis appeared. Nietzsche however had suffered hallucinations since he was 24.

According to the philosopher Eckhart Tolle, **scientific dogmas are collective mental prisons** into which one likes to squeeze "because they …convey a feeling of safety and the false sensation: "I know". Freud was wrong and only thought he knew. Let us therefore not immediately postulate the Sacco-Syndrome as a dogma and let us not claim religion to be at the root of every mental illness. How intensively **our Churches' concept of sin** provides our psychiatrists with work (without realizing it) shall be discussed here: The 260 clinical cases which Freud mentions in his "Psychopathology of Every-Day Life" can be categorized into four different "sins" according to the Sermon of the Mount: 57 x insincerity, 122 x selfishness, 39 x impurity, 42 x coldness (according to Tournier). Inventing the concept of sin is a clever move of the Churches, the only thing is, one has to wait a very long time for potential forgiveness. That is different with simple "guilt" which can generally be settled during one's lifetime. Also, a believer, when considering the word "sin", immediately thinks of the "mercy" which is necessary for the forgiveness of sin. The reason being that without the only potentially granted mercy which is sung about in the more than 100 songs, the sinner, according to the current official Church doctrine, will end up in eternal hell. The modern cleric governs with the concept of "potential mercy". They find a God of Love, in their words a wellness God, unpleasant, because he does not allow them to satisfy their own thoughts of revenge. Our Churches claim that tiny trespasses (stealing an apple off God) are in themselves gigantic sins, and this trick serves as breeding ground for the every-day mental diseases. In view of this fact, how can anyone dispute that we are trapped in religious Middle Ages.

Fear of God, fear of hell

A term for fear must bear strong reference to what is meant. With its emphasis purely on genitals, fear of castration does not have that in this country. We internists are also only to ready to do without terms like oral and anal sadism. It would certainly be possible to define more exactly our sense of basic fear as "FoP" (fear of parents), so that it becomes more accessible for all doctors. It would also be possible to misinterpret "Parent Fear" as a fear the parents have, just as "divine fear" could possibly mean fear of a God. Using FoP, the term is sufficiently described. Analogous to that, fear of God is more adequately referred to as "FoG". I herewith introduce these abbreviations into the nomenclature.

It is more likely that a God who has been invented by the writers of the bible becomes angry when a child masturbates than that the natural father does. He who in the end punishes, castrates or shortens the penis, is also the wrathful, equally sexually timid as sexless, God, and not the sexually active father. The invented "God" finally wants the circumcision to take place which the rabbi only performs or has to perform. By giving orders for the "partial castration" – circumcision – "God" castrates. This is done to young children (to Jewish children when they are eight days old) without anaesthesia or local anaesthetic and represents a considerable trauma ordered by "Jahwe" which is remembered for a while.

Fear of circumcision (Jewish children)

Post-operational" care takes several days even weeks. Numerous deaths are described as having occurred in the old days, e. g. tuberculosis, beginning on the little penis, which the rabbi would put into his infected mouth in order to gather the blood. In animal medicine, these methods have long been banned. In "Serenity and other human possibilities" " …", Suhrkamp, Leo Rangell tells of a repeated circumcision on a 12year-old patient which his mother had had done because he had masturbated. "Cruelly and forcibly" the doctor had performed this. According to Rangell, this trauma resulted in fears of castration which lasted into adulthood and made psychoanalysis necessary. In this particular case, the concept fear of castration even makes sense to me.

In the Near East, a cruel version existed: The skin on the boy's penis and testicles was stripped and into the wound salt would be rubbed. It was always God as the giver of orders who had to take the blame for such rituals and who bore full responsibility when complications occurred. That was practical. The matter does prove, however, that we human beings are the craziest animal species on this earth.

Circumcision as trauma was one reason to make the inventor of psychoanalysis, S. Freud, as sexually driven as one can derive from his theories on analysis, which can be related to human beings who have not been circumcised. It must be horrendous for Jewish children to have to attend the circumcision of their younger brothers.

"Hands off his foreskin" one wants to shout out to Jahwe. For me personally, that would be no celebration. Anything insane and brutal however is easier to put up with if it is labelled a celebration by the Church. With "God" we even like going to war. Freud was also considered to be driven by sexual interpretations due to the following fact: Young, pretty women were expected to suddenly speak completely openly and as if they were lying in bed about their sexual habits, dreams and fantasies, and they did this as happily as lightly dressed during summertime. The therapists often sat at the head end. That way, a potential erection (even therapists are only human) would not become apparent.

Sexuality – a sin?

In 1938, Freud writes: "The key last reason for all inhibitions of intellect and work seems to be inhibition of childhood masturbation. Maybe, however, it goes deeper …" At this point one could definitely quote fear of hell as the deepest reason. It is "God's" actual ruthless punishment of unrepented or confessed masturbation which the Catholic Church again declared a free ride to eternal hell only in 1975. Freud actually did have an inkling of the Sacco-Syndrome. He realises in the end that the "super-ego often unfolds a harshness for which the real parents have often not set an example", and he had a hunch which I call the "Freudian hunch":

that the moral dimension is not acquired but has been implanted by a higher body ….." Here, the atheist is exposed as a believer: He claims Oedipus, in spite of actually being guilt-free, feels guilty anyway and therefore punishes himself. So Freud ends up in the mental sewer of sin, God of revenge, fear of hell and ecclesiogenous masochism with his Oedipus after all. Oedipus castrates and punishes himself in order to prevent having to go to hell, instead of being happy to have had such pleasant and fruitful hours in bed with his attractive mother. Instead, he dazzles himself, hoping that in doing so, God would punish him less severely. Convinced that he has "sinned" badly twice, he overrates the appropriateness of the sentence for this sacrifice. As the eye is a very sensitive organ, he chooses his eyes. If we found ourselves in a similar situation, we would, if absolutely unavoidable, rather brand-mark our bottom. Incidentally, the Koran is also familiar with sensitivity of the eyes: Non-believers enter eternal fire "eyes first". Not until after that does the back get put onto the permanent grill (see Sure 4, "Women" ("Die Weiber").

His father did not castrate poor Oedipus because he was not able to! He was already dead. He had died as a result of the accident mentioned above. Does one fear the dead because they might carry out a penis amputation – or more likely the God who is declared to be alive and terrible? Freud was once more hot on the heels of understanding the Sacco-Syndrome, the diseases caused by insidious religious beliefs or superstition (see my book of the same name). It is more simple and scientifically correct to replace the term "fear of castration" with "fear of hell". Then one is on the right track with the greatest fear of boys and girls (in almost all religions). Religions were, as we know, primarily thought up in order to satisfy the human need to feel protected in this cruel world. This basic need is abused by leading clerics by making extreme threats, because they believe that they have themselves and their Church to feed. Great things are always very easy, as is the theory of relativity. It is actually in principle totally straightforward. What the cleric actually believes, must, however, become a subject of investigation.

"Forbidden" masturbation rightly plays an important part in classic psychoanalysis, see Leo Rangell. Being caught at filial love with the mother (or – in today's language – the effort to beat the father in the succession of generations) or in the process of masturbating is, on the one hand harmless (the father will not and may not even castrate him or apply any other such form of violence), on the other hand, however, extremely dangerous: The other part of the super-ego, our God-Ego or Church-Ego, is on bad terms with sex. The clerics instill remorse in the believers who are dependent on them in confession and forgiveness to the extreme point of threatening with hell and purgatory. That works very well. Earning hard cash through achieving power is the aim. Human beings however do not need a living God to form a conscience, after all, the old Greeks had a conscience without Zeus ever having lived. On the other hand, baptized believers were responsible for Auschwitz.

Save us from the fire of hell

In order to develop their part of the super-ego, the Church-ego, the Church uses its most talented people. With a smile on their face, men in black speak on K-TV about their God of Fire. From 16:00 to 16:20, they pray to Jesus with the trembling children: "Save us from the fire of hell." The Protestant Church also threatens children officially by telling them that their "body and soul" will burn in hell if they do not repent. That is organized terror, regulated in §241 of the Criminal Code.

The European Convention of Human Rights forbids all (!) forms of threats of violence, too. Furthermore, our **Protection of the Constitution** has recently begun to expect the Churches to obey existing laws. In front of children, the men in black say that one must pray diligently for the "tormented in purgatory", as that could shorten their pains there! The word "torture" however, is strictly avoided, it evokes the German Illness 1933-45 too painfully. With such programmes, which are strangely tolerated by our supposedly critical society, it is suggested to our young ones that fire in hell actually exists. It is of great importance that the term purgatory remains. Here, fire is the clerics' favorite word. To every rule, however, there is an exception. That goes for clerics, doctors, sociologists and psychologists.

The safest sex is no sex

Bible-God himself does not seem to exercise sex, and in his bible he has draconian sentences at his fingertips for "illicit sex", even to the extent of commanding to burn alive (!) women who have become unchaste, even those completely oblivious that they have become involved. This command the clerics would obey happily. In his supposedly so harmless sermon on the mount, Bible-Jesus recommends tearing out an eye of a husband who only so much as throws a desiring glance at another woman passing by, this being preferable to going to hell forever. So, in Christianity, the sole desire and the committed sin become one. The Christian God, so our Churches believe, have their cameras set up everywhere, in our bedrooms and even in our brains. In that respect, our God's predecessor, or fellow competitor, Zeus, was still completely different. The Gods of Mount Olympus were sexually extremely active, whereas Mary's sheet remained spotless.

Therefore, in the fundamentalist bible, the enemy can be found in our children's suppressed prime fears. They are made to believe that masturbation is a sin, punished severely by an unpredictable "God". The parent or legal guardian may rebuke but not cruelly punish the child, as this would be against the law. The youth welfare department would be called in after a bloody castration, discovered during a change of nappies. Even today, the Church God, however, is allowed to apply torture in order to punish, in hell and also to children under 14 years of age, who have not yet reached the age of criminal responsibility. After all, hell is by no means declared child-free: Only the conception of a pre-hell for children who have not been baptized has recently been abolished. Allegedly, there was never such a thing. In this respect one had "been mistaken".

A bad year: 2010

The fact that Churches are officially hostile towards sex is confirmed daily with their bible and by the way they deal with issues like homosexuality, extramarital intercourse, divorce, contraception, our priests' celibacy etc. Unofficially however, things are very different as far as pastoral sex with children is concerned: Divided up into groups, priests swarmed boys' dormitories. On suspicion of hemorrhoids, they inspected the boys' rectums by inserting something other than a forefinger. Those are known as the "Kloster Ettaler Doktorspiele" ("doctors and nurses at Ettal Monastery"), an example of the unscrupulous behavior of a large number of the clerics which took place without permission of the General Medical Council. In 2010, we are amazed to read that, under protection and with the approval of the Church and the Vatican Religious Congregation under Cardinal Ratzinger, clerics had been inserting their erect penises into just about any imaginable opening their little pupils had to offer.

The child molester is "loved by the Pope", therefore the business was "very sensitive", said Cardinal Ratzinger, when he let go the Mexican mass-paedophile Father Maciel ("possibly even 100 boys"). Ratzinger imposed maintaining "absolute silence" to the outside world (Source: Stern 15/2010). A child-molesting priest, however, is okay to molest more than everyone else, due to his great relationship with God. After all, he has sacrificed his whole life and is consumed with considerable privation. Two priests can, in order to avoid hell, confess to each other although this may have practical advantages, it has eliminated the supposed holiness of confession forever.

Jesus is free of sins

On December 29, 1975, the Catholic Religious Congregation reaffirmed that masturbation is a deathly sin sending one to hell. This happens to be the definition of deadly sin. The same goes for homosexual deeds – at the same time, an estimated 60% of all priests are homosexual. They often take up this profession because by doing so they are not confronted so easily with the question of the whereabouts of a wife. A friend of mine told me that when becoming aware of his affection towards the male sex, he felt he had to make a choice between: this "religion" – or his own personal emotions. In this conflict, his choice had fallen on the latter. Well done! "Nearly every child will masturbate more or less frequently at different stages in his/her life", says **Dr. Gisela Eberlein** correctly in "Ängste gesunder Kinder" (Fears of Healthy Children). Even toddlers are sexually active. Now, just like the practicing of masturbation later on, this activity is of course completely free of guilt and sin and is an integral part of playing and joie de vivre. Monkeys and dogs do it, even in public, and entirely lacking feelings of guilt or shame or fears of a hell. It is also unlikely that sensible Mary would have been constantly stopping her son from doing it. After all, why would she, a Holy Mother, want to so strictly and forcibly forbid such a natural thing? **Given that Jesus is considered free of sins, masturbation can, therefore, not be a sin.** In this respect, the Churches have again been mistaken. To err is clerical. Jesus is said to have been married or engaged, and why ever not? Documents about this are kept strictly under lock and key in Israel. Why?

S. Freud reports: "In analysis, it is particularly important that the child is helped to remember its own forgotten sexual activity as well as the interference through the adults which put an end to it." With peoples belonging to "lower culture", says Freud, "children's sexuality seems to have been set free". Is it not, however, more plausible that in this case the Jewish and Christian beliefs which declare children's innocent play a sin, even a deathly sin – punished with death – represent the "lower culture"? What is culture anyway? Is it on a par with humanity or with inhumanity? In fact, a child's sexual experiences play an important part in a disease it has developed. This is not due to fear of castration but to fear of hell.

Back in the Middle Ages

Eugen Drewermann mentions the Vatikan's "crazy fanaticism" which commands us to believe that sexuality is allowed solely for the purpose of procreation (i. e. three to five times in a lifetime) and during only one marriage. Otherwise in case of death it is punishment in hell, says Drewermann with an exclamation mark. Today, in 2010 (!), representatives of the Catholic Church are seriously discussing whether to abolish the doctrine excluding a divorcee who has remarried from Holy Communion – which is considered the only way to have her sins forgiven and to be delivered from eternal hell. Should they actually dare this significant step away from the Middle Ages?

As around 1900, the Church representatives were proclaiming with much greater force that masturbation would lead directly into hell, the children suffering from this fear appeared to the psychiatrists to be severely ill: "Greyish-pale, earth-colored complexion, pale lips, bluish eyelids, tired-looking skin, perspiration, shaking, weakness of the back, dull pain in thighs and calves, stuttering, weakness of the voice, irksomeness, listlessness as regards play and work, hysteria, later also male inability" etc. (Die Welt, November 6, 2010). Even S. Freud had his doubts regarding health issues: Diverse disorders could occur if childish auto-eroticism was not completely overcome.

Since sex reformer Nina Hagen's masturbation performance on TV, however, we know better. It is actually a healthy business. Maybe, however, the diagnosing psychiatrists were ill. **Claire Goll**, Rilke's girlfriend, wrote: "Carl Gustav Jung … was however, just like all psychiatrists I have ever known, insane and megalomaniac in his own way". She mentions the **"metaphysical mire"** in which psychiatrists "so often lose their footing. This **occupational disease** holds great dangers for the equilibrium of those who are on to the mental derailments of others". If Ms. Goll were to be internist today, she would also be declared paranoid-psychotic by psychiatrists, who would try to kill her faculty to criticize with psychiatric drugs. However, Claire was just as far away from being paranoid as I am. She was a keen observer and recognized a mania with psychiatrists who considered themselves specialists for the treatment of manias. Of course, the delusions of grandeur she diagnosed only served to cover up a feeling of inferiority which again represents a denial of reality (*ref. W Schmidbauer, "Hilflose Helfer", rororo*).

Fear of God instead of fear of parents

In psychoanalysis, the term "fear of castration" can be freely replaced with the term "fear of parents" and "fear of God". Freud's fear of castration is also more likely to have been fear of God: Only too obviously did he avoid the central issues Last Judgment and Hell which our clerics, after all, profess beyond any doubt to be religious certainties. 50 Church songs are about hell, 50 are about the devil working there for "Jesus". Clerics believe that they need fairy tales like the all-deciding Last Judgment to exist. However, how can the Bible-God, who is responsible for the Flood and who is Head of Hell, possibly judge or even condemn emulators?

Incidentally: What is the loss of two testicles or any other parental punishment compared with eternal torture in hell? Weighing up the scale of cruelty, how does Parent-Ego compare with God-ego or Church-ego? Do men not nowadays even undergo castration voluntarily for family planning purposes?

Who, however, would really like to voluntarily go into Jesus' eternity soup cauldron that children are, for example, made to look at in the Paderborn Dome? The Bishop there, Bishop Becker, wants the little ones to see this altar piece **"as early on in life as possible"**, since this would pave the way for them to become **"especially sensitive"**. That is true. I then wrote to Mr. Becker asking him for a change and received no answer, in spite of him being perfectly aware of the fact that children believe everything the Churches put in front of them.

Bible-Jesus demanding in his sermon on the mount to tear out one's own eye or even to chop off one's arm, should the situation arise, is not only extremely pathological, but also the root of disease (therefore, Bible-Jesus urgently needs to go and see a psychiatrist). These demands represent cause, origin and instructions for masochistic behavior with believers, which used to be: becoming a monk, the belt of repentance, asceticism and burning oneself to death. Today, Church-induced masochism is hidden in "endogenous depression" or the "fear of fear" and of which as yet our psychiatrists are completely unaware. This is about to change. What will also change is the fact that therapists so like to regularly blame parents or even the patients themselves for the mental illness.

Autism and the biggest fear

Fear of hell causes a variety of diseases. The thought or fear of hell can frighten children so strongly that they completely withdraw from this world in Church-induced autism. At birth, an autistic will already have experienced nine months of life, during which he/she will have absorbed all the mother's fears. The autist Birger Sellin heals himself by writing a liberating book: about hell, eternal damnation and the fire in which an autist will always burn. Equally, the patient suffering from a schizophrenia occurring later on, prefers to establish a more tolerable world of his/her own. Autism and schizophrenia are an escape from what is unbearable and, as research with twins shows, not hereditary. Only intelligence and/or sensitivity as a condition for mental disease are hereditary. Being indoctrinated with fear of hell can cause addictions (to alcohol, smoking, drugs, eating disorders, diabetes) as well as ADS and diverse psychosomatic disorders.

One is allowed to ask children

Ought one not, in order to support Freud's Theory of Sexuality, devote a study to asking preschool and school children questions like: "What are testicles? Where are they? What would it mean to you if one day they disappeared? Are you frightened of losing them or your penis in one way or another? If so: How frightened are you? What do you think could cause a loss of these organs? In contrast to the usual psychiatric silence (the known and educated ("Yes, yes, hm, hm"), questions can quickly open the door to the subconscious. Children must also have questions put to them concerning their natural father. Is one afraid of him? Is one worried he may harm one in any way? Does one really wish to have the parent of the opposite sex all to oneself in every way? Can the father-son relationship (or daughter respectively) cause some kind of stronger fear with the child? A fear strong enough to cause addiction, depression or even psychosis?

Similar questions must be put to small children about hell: Do you know what that is, hell? Do, in your opinion, fires burn there? Why do fires burn there? Do you believe everything it says in the bible? Can you imagine that those are God's words? Is the bible holy? Do you believe that the paintings on the ceilings of Churches represent the truth? Is it allowed to doubt what is said in the bible? Is it allowed to contradict "God" or the cleric? Are you afraid of them? Can the story of the Flood be true? Did you feel sorry for the animals when you first heard the story of the Flood? Did this God frighten you to death? Have psychoanalysts ever addressed such or similar questions to children, clients or themselves? The psychiatrist who examined me had to think for a while before she was able to answer my question whether she believed in hell. Whoever needs to reflect this question however, is bound to believe a little in this alleged eternal concentration camp, and since Auschwitz, we certainly do not believe that God or Jesus could possibly want to start operating such a place.

In "Das Christentum und die Angst" („Christianity and Fear"), p. 272, O. Pfister tells us: „ ….by establishing strict moral and religious commands and bans, by imprinting horrifying thoughts in the minds of children from an early age on, by translating lifeforce into paths of obsessional neurosis, the Church created living conditions that inevitably resulted in extreme anxiety." The entire power of the Church is based on anxiety and authority. A neuroticizing system finally lives off the neurosis as does a virus of the disease, says Eugen Drewermann, who draws up the Pfister quote. On June 8, 2011, there was the following news on TV: What led innocent human beings into destruction was "not religious belief". Correct! On a park bench in Hamburg/Blankenese someone had written: "Religious beliefs that threaten children with eternal damnation are filthy organized sadists". This is a rather drastic way of putting it, but the park bench knew what it was telling us about.

Even if the toddler does not yet know all the verses of the bible, the person responsible for its upbringing has memorized the bible together with a childhood belief. The location in the brain is called super-ego or conscience. During verbal and non-verbal contact between parent or parental guide, "God" or ideas of God are translated as super-ego directly onto the child. Impossible to claim that toddlers know nothing about belief, do not understand anything or do not know how (cruel) God is. They are weaned on this, whether it is the mother's intention or not. Furthermore, religious feelings of guilt are translated "to the seventh level" – a lifelong punishment. This is how long it takes for God-Ego thoughts to cease to be handed down through the generations. Also, not until then is an atheist family truly atheist. This is also the reason why the blasphemer Dostojewski never met a non-believer. Really, every atheist should know of leftovers of religious beliefs in him. If not, I consider him at a certain risk.

Psychiatrists and their fear of God

The term "fear of hell" ("Höllenangst") is almost unknown in "modern" psychiatry and sociology ("Höhlenangst?" ("Fear of caves"?) psychiatrists often enquire). Such a thing is not talked about. Hell is taboo. Only when a cleric seriously talks or preaches of heaven or hell, everyone listens, impressed or even affected. However, when a doctor talks easily and freely about this central issue of our religious belief, and therefore that of our children, he has to undergo a medical examination and is officially declared paranoid. Nobody would dare to define our German Pope as insane when he writes that Catholics share a belief in hell with "the Protestant friends" (in "Einführung in das Christentum" ("Introduction to Christianity")). Were the thought of hell not collectively suppressed and therefore contained in our collective subconscious, one would surely not put children into this world who, if they got on the wrong side of Jesus, would have to suffer eternal torture. Would one not prefer always using a condom for reasons of love of children and one's neighbor?

According to our psychiatrists, threatening with hell is not supposed to cause anxieties? In this respect, psychiatrists, on a superficial level, make themselves look extremely ridiculous, just like the colleague first judging me in the meeting of the Chamber. As a psychiatrist (!), he was not even able to name the deepest fear of human being, the fear of (eternal) torture. His unqualified remark was that in Germany torture hardly existed. He ignored more than 100 million bibles and the more than 100 million hymn books officially announcing eternal torture in hell through Jesus to the child, causing this deepest anxiety.

After all, fear that the world may come to an end exists without this ever having actually happened. He ignored analyst Tilman Moser's unchallenged insight, which I submitted, who knows of **millions of children ill with church-induced anxiety** and who writes books about them, like the bestseller "Gottesvergiftung" ("Poisoned by God"). He ignored the alleged knowledge of the Vatikan in the year 2000, which I submitted, that in a hell already functioning today, there was such torture that one could **die from sheer horror** purely by watching, if one was not saved by "God's almighty power. In this way, the Churches poison not only our children with their lies, but the real God himself. They allow God no dignity and do not shy away from the (according to Dawkins) worst possible form of child abuse: emotional abuse. This is often combined with sexual abuse in the following way: A patient of mine was threatened with having to go to hell if she told her mother about the rape which had taken place. These kind of threats were **a known fact**, so I was told during a visit to Tilmann Moser in a Stadtmission in southern Germany. That is bound to put you off religion, hopefully this goes for you too, dear reader.

As, however, I use the term fear of hell (or Sacco-Syndrome) – this is how the written argument of the authority of my license to practice medicine goes – and as I accused the Churches of emotional violence (!), I was forced to undergo psychiatric examinations in the institutional outpatient department. There, I was declared as "paranoid-psychotic", the reasons given being that I was too suspicious towards psychiatrists and was preoccupied with thoughts of hell and that this was not social. Without my permission and partly giving away my identity (full initials, full address), the authority for the license to practice had, to be on the safe side, also informed the clinic of the diagnosis they had guessed on as a result of a pre-examination with the Medical Association. During the above-mentioned pre-examination, the circumstances of which were unlawful (coercion, no legal information, invited to no more than one "talk"), the Vice President of the Federal Medical Association, Dr. med. Goesmann, confirmed the results which my investigations of the Churches had yielded and said she had even left the Catholic Church because of the atrocities described by me.

According to the lawyer of the Chamber, however, this statement was not allowed to be included in the protocol, as it supported my views and not those of the Medical Chamber, which, after all, is committed to denounce and prevent atrocities it hears about – even if our Churches themselves are the penetrators. The official comment was that it had been a personal comment of the Vice President's. Silence from the side of the Chamber was the answer to my question whether the Vice President (with an additional qualification in psychotherapy) would now also have to undergo a psychiatric examination.

Furthermore, this public body could suddenly not remember the oath of silence which had been agreed upon for that evening and immediately broken the next day. Fortunately however, I had of course made sure I was accompanied by a credible witness for the talk.

What she also did not tell me was that in 2008, the head of a psychiatric institute had reported me to the police as a response to the letter I had written him, answering an invitation to a congress. In it I pointed out that one would have to consider whether psychiatrists might themselves be subconsciously frightened of hell. He found this "bizarre". What followed were extensive secret police investigations about me in order to "avert danger". These investigations involved the State Criminal Police and local interviews. The colleague had warned the police that I could be as dangerous as the shooter at Winnenden and therefore likely to kill 18 people and to be in possession of a weapon. The question was put whether I was a hunter! He was afraid of me. Thank God, however, the police was not paranoid and did not lock me up. The head of the investigations was of the opinion that the colleague had "not been objective". To my amazement, only the authority of license to practice placed this single and strange charge in the centre of its accusations against me.

Criticism of psychiatrists

It can be concluded that criticism is not popular with psychiatrists, as they have usually suffered emotional injury as children, from which strong, lifelong feelings of inferiority result, which are kept behind a mask of supposed strength. This is known to all of us non-psychiatrists The psychiatrists themselves, however, have not yet individually internalized this aspect. Consequence of the investigations was the strict regulation by the authority that I must see a psychiatrist on a regular monthly basis and take drugs with a dampening effect, which, according to the package insert can have considerable side effects and which may result even in death. Thus assenting, psychiatrists as well as the authority with license to practice, accept that I may possibly die as a result of the treatment. According to the authority, I should take the medication purely as for the sake of "prevention". Even though I had not yet done anything wrong with any patient, such an event might yet occur …."Outrageous" was my solicitor's comment, and he is right. My impression was simply that it was their intention to silence me with medicinal chains and stop me from taking any further action (reporting any more people/institutions to the police).

What impresses me is the carelessness with which scholars of law, when confronted with religion, risk losing their own certificate to practice. It is one of the many examples of how powerful emotions can cause common sense to fail. Also, the way the Flood, which allegedly truly happened, is celebrated in protestant kindergartens as being an act of some kind of justice, demonstrates such a loss of common sense and, in addition, is strictly forbidden here, according to §131 of the Criminal Code. Here, German law is quite correct in stating that no Holocaust is just and that there is nothing to applaud.

Delinquency, violence and the fear of hell

I am, however, not so very alone with my criticism of psychiatrists. The book "Kriminalsoziologie", F. Sack und R. König, Akademische Verlagsgesellschaft Frankfurt a. M., shows that psychiatry cannot satisfactorily explain what actually causes delinquency and violence. The fault found with psychiatry is that it speaks of what is "normal" without even being able to define the term. "Babylonian confusion" as regards diagnostic terms is demonstrated by drawing up examples, and it is said that the psychiatrists' personality, emotional set-up and own bias determine their diagnosis. Psychiatrists are reported to be "extremely careless" and only "insufficiently informed".

They are suspected of classifying patients arbitrarily, subjectively and invalidly into "oral erotics, oral sadists, anal erotics and anal sadists". A mentioned psychiatric institution comes to a specific diagnosis in 37% of all cases, a comparable institution reaches none at all. Regrettably, "legislative and executive powers" respected and trusted psychiatrists and believed that their statements were "checked and true". This however was "definitely not the case"!

The lawyer of the executive "authority for the license to practice" apparently did not read this book. Thank God he cannot yet take away the license to practice from sociologists or even force them to take medication. It is therefore adequate and essential to be suspicious of psychiatrists. Sack's investigations culminate in the sentence that there is no proof that psychiatrists "consistently came to better judgments about people than the layman". Therefore, it makes sense that the authority for the license to practice took the precaution to inform the clinic responsible for my treatment in writing of my suspected diagnosis. After all, they did not want anything to go wrong with the finding of the diagnosis. However, that is of course illegal deceitfulness, as it took place without my consent. And is therefore an act of criminal offence in office.

Apart from disease of course, delinquency is caused by our evil and harmful disreligion. In this respect, evil causes evil. A child who, for one reason or another, is considered the black sheep of the family or at school and does not feel loved, will see him- or herself on the waiting list for hell under the strict eyes of his teacher of religious studies or of the clerics. He will believe that he belongs to 50% of all human beings who end up in the fire there as it is depicted in the Church paintings. In this deeply emotional situation, he will develop aspects of extreme emotional disturbance, be discontented, feel inferior and develop feelings of guilt. He will follow impulses to find recognition by joining a gang, substitute lack of satisfaction through living out anger in destruction and watch violent and pornographic programmes in order to vent aggression.

As the child's subconscious knows that he/she will go to hell anyway, the family's as well as the Church's efforts to regulate him will be to no avail. Nothing matters to the youth anymore, he becomes a problem. According to Durkheim, the result is a lack of norms as a reaction to the "realization" that he will be punished in an eternal hell endlessly and excessively and unfairly. If it does not pave the way to depression, the consequence of such maximum frustration will naturally be maximum aggression. According to **R. K. Merton**, retreat could also be the result. As an example, he draws on "**autism**", i. e. child schizophrenia, and is in this respect more qualified than our psychiatrists of today. Of course, the borderline syndrome and adults' schizophrenia are in most cases Church-induced. C. G. Jung wrote his doctoral thesis on psychotherapy and schizophrenia and classifies them as being caused by experience and consequently as **neurosis with a tendency to retreat**. Merton writes further about "tramps, psychopaths, chronic drinkers and addicts" who try to reduce the extent of their suffering with their behavior. This also includes "adipositas" in children and adults which lead to diabetes, psychosomatic conditions and the ADS syndrome. Nietzsche and Max Scheler mention that patients could react with feelings of "resentment", confused "feelings of hatred, jealousy and hostility".

The biologist Prof. M. F. A. Montagu views most crimes as a "reaction to any form of lack of personal security", and the ones who most vehemently cause feelings of insecurity are doubtlessly our Churches. Montagu goes on to say: "It is not the individual who commits the crime but society". In our case, this means the Churches with their constant threats of outrageous maximum violence.

"Ecclesiogenous neurosis" one used to be allowed to call the consequences of this violence. Today, due to the influence of the Churches (after all frequently responsible for psychiatric clinics and therefore our psychiatrists' employers), this term is not allowed to be used as official diagnosis anymore, since it does not appear in the diagnosis key ICD-10 anymore. It is not surprising that, according to scientific research, psychotherapy of prison inmates generally does not achieve any improvement: The delinquents' basic fear is not addressed by the hell-phobic psychiatrists. I was also not able to find the word "hell" in the above-mentioned 500-page book "Kriminalsoziologie". It does not appear in the 19-page index. Just like our psychiatry, sociology seems to be married to the Church and to protect it diligently but completely unjustifiably.

Guilty for an actual death by torture?

In his book "Sozialisierung und Erziehung", ("Socialisation and Upbringing"), Beltz Verlag, educationalist Helmut Fend writes: Moral norms are often justified with religion and therefore have special sanctions allocated to them (e. g. punishment ....through death). I could not discover the word "hell" in the book. At least Fend mentions that sanctions lead to social control. The forms of discovery (absolute duty to repent), judgment (Last Judgment as certainty of belief) and punishment (eternal hell) are perfectly formalized and institutionalized in the Church. It is therefore the Church disciplining with the greatest severity. Its power to sanction, represented by the eternal punishments it threatens with, is doubtless not only the most severe but unfortunately also the most effective form of social control. Clerics would exploit the child's in most cases extreme fear of physical pain by threatening with torture. Dear reader, here we are dealing with people more intelligent than you and I. At least I do attempt with my IQ to keep up a little with the basics: By applying diverse techniques, the clerics use their intelligence to extinguish our little ones' ability to criticize, convincing them up to a mature adult age that they are to blame personally for their "sins" (and this explicitly post mortal!) for a death by torture that a small number of people committed 2000 years ago.

By doing so, it is disregarding §19 of the Criminal Code by accusing our children of complicity with the intention of causing excessive feelings of guilt, and in fact succeeding in doing so in the child's subconscious. This guilt they are talked into is then forgiven in a Communion which is declared holy. However, Rilke already knows: "Poison and embers" inoculate our children during Communion. It is the poison of this maximum guilt they have been made to believe in and the embers of the fear of hell in case of not being forgiven for this non-existent guilt. How can a child be happy with itself having been talked into feeling guilty for an actual death by torture? Holy Communion should be allowed to be celebrated simply as a farewell meal and no longer as a guilt trap. By the way, Jesus' condemnation and death were pre-programmed when he demanded to reign over the Jewish people with neither an army to support him and nor an accompanying letter from his father. Even today, there is a lifelong sentence for such a crime in Germany ("high treason"). Scientists puzzle why to this day deep psychologists cannot express any type of criticism of Bible-Jesus. The reason for these lies, amongst other things, with the limitless gratitude towards Christ because the Churches claim that he died on the cross on behalf of all of us. In order to forgive the sins, all God would have needed to do was to clap his hands, furthermore, this allegation suggests a cruel and totally unnecessary murder of his own son …

The word "holy" is deliberately used by Churches in order to stabilize especially questionable things such as "Holy See" or "Holy Spirit". They also succeed via suggestion technology to declare someone as limitlessly merciful or even as impersonated love whom they have presented to our children as the perpetrator of the global genocide, the Fire God of Sodom and Gomorrah and head of hell. In any case, there is no book that is more hostile towards children and Jesus than the bible. In Luke 17 for example, Luke has Jesus' claim that the alleged "redeemer" was planning two more holocausts, one using water, the next one using fire. We enlightened human beings are surprised at the apostle and wonder about what motivates him to spread such lies about someone who is Love and, being dead, cannot defend himself. In "Vielfalt und Profil ("Diversity and Profile") Neuenkirchener, 1999, Prof. Dr. Rolf Rendtorff writes something strange: Love of one's neighbor counts as being Christian, God (or Christ) himself, however, was himself so to speak not Christian, in spite of having been baptized. The "crucial point" as regards Christianity was "not to take revenge oneself but to leave this to God. "Revenge is mine, I will repay, thus says the Lord" (Romans 12, 19, New (!) Testament). Church people often hope that those will be tortured in hell who did not lead such an abstinent, God-fearing and pious life as they have. They hope for a "just" compensation to balance out their sacrifices to life and do not see the beam in their own eyes.

Through suggestion technology and authoritarian behavior the Churches also manage to declare someone who died on the cross has come back to life again. Unfortunately however, at present, the crucified one was for some reason relatively shy of the media. Mind you, sometimes samples of his fresh blood would appear.

It is said that Jesus' blood was tested and his blood group was AB. Furthermore, saints had seen him several times and it was possible for the religious ordinary people to "speak" to him, so it says.

In a further effort to oppose suggestion technology with common sense, let me point out the following: The Church's advertisement that God has the so-called almighty power to save believers from the greatest earthly misery was forfeited at the latest with the existence of the torture chambers of Auschwitz.

The Church's bogus argument claiming that the fact that God had "granted us the freedom" (even to torture) dismisses him, the Almighty our alleged Creator, from his duty to have regard of the welfare of children, can only be convincing through means of suggestion. Let us better stick to it: God is Love and as such not almighty. We are his hands. If we internalize this, Bible-God's alleged murdering after Eve stole the apple off the tree will also be identified as earmarked for a special purpose.

Its aim is to frighten children by demonstrating to them "God's" absolute small-mindedness and pettiness: Unjustifiably, he brutally punishes his daughter Eve's first small act of defiance, using global kinship liability up to this day. It would have done this God some good to read a year or so of pedagogy at university.

Was there any such thing as paradise in those days? Did not Eve's vegetarian snake devour her toads alive and, considering such cruelty in nature, can a God feel pleased with himself and expect gratitude? Therefore, let us say farewell to the superstition that we are creations. We just simply exist. Let us make the best of that.

What our children need is a new religion

During the period of Enlightenment, ending in 1918, one did not accept this from our clerics anymore. However, times have changed again. Fundamentalism (and the Middle Ages) has returned. Being Christian however works quite well without it, without the humility which is permanently demanded by the Churches in their own self-interest and even with common sense and science and strictly rejecting any belief of miracles, bibles, angels or spirits – including the so-called Holy Spirit who has no sense of humor whatsoever and who is the most evil of all spirits. According to an alleged word of Jesus, the Churches proclaim that whoever sins against this spirit will end up directly in hell without any compassion from Jesus. During her theological studies, my sister however already knows better: "Love is the Holy Spirit", she says. She, my patients who are believers and I can actually imagine a Christianity completely without a hell and a devil, those Church's instruments of power! And as historical access to Jesus is denied us intentionally, we would do right – and our children justice – to simply define him and, at the same time, God and the Holy Spirit. All three are unconditional love.

Spoken by anyone but the clerics, the term hell seems to terrify psychiatrists. Why ever might that be the case? They sense threat, fear and sometimes feel "deadly bored" and then angry, and during their training, they learn it is better to change the subject or to interrupt the talk or end the relationship. The term "hell" immediately leads to the thoughts stalling, at the same time preventing any notion of the potential damage hell-sermons can cause to the souls of small children and making it impossible to seriously criticize the Church. To my surprise, my examiner called me in to her institute a second time.

This second examination was to find out whether I was "doing missionary work" in my practice. Obviously, she had heard something dreadful about me. In fact, the Church (!) does send patients to me for psychotherapy, whom psychotherapists have refused to treat. A therapist I was forced to see for further treatment was apparently also told to warn me to talk neither about the Church nor its mistakes and the resulting diseases. Interestingly, at the same time, he honestly stated that he himself had been affected so badly by Church-induced neurosis that he found it impossible to talk about religious feelings of guilt. Due to his anxiety, he had not been able to become a fully functional therapist. For the purpose of comparison: A trained car mechanic must, after all, also have the courage to open the bonnet to take a look at the engine in case of trouble.

Freud killed his God Jahwe

As far as receiving my license to practice was concerned, I became very busy playing down my activities in this respect and realized, that being a doctor is not a liberal profession anymore. My fundamental rights of freedom of action and of religion were being interfered with and the intention was to simply prevent me from having clarifying talks with patients. I was expected to join the general psychiatrists' neurosis but did not feel at all like complying with it. How this general neurosis comes about is easily explained: With his sentence "Religion is insanity", Freud killed his God Jahwe only in his surface consciousness.

Without realizing it himself however, he remained faithful to his Jewish religion in his core self. After that, Freud's subconscious did not allow him any more "sins" against Jahwe. Enough was enough. Such "wantonness" would have been to openly criticize religion and to explain to the patients that their illnesses were a direct result of the crimes committed by the Churches. Instead, Freud fainted when murder of God was mentioned. The most spectacular one was committed during the Psychoanalytical Congress in Munich 1913. Speaker Jung was just explaining that the sons of pharaohs had regularly disempowered or killed their fathers (Gods) and then replaced them by empowering themselves. They had, however, not inaugurated a new religion. "At this instance, Freud slipped from his chair unconscious", said Jung. In Freud's opinion, this neurosis of his needed treating.

Was this fainting a "coincidence" or not? Of course not. The fainting in Munich 1913 had been preceded under analogous circumstances 1912 in Munich and by unconsciousness in the Bremen "Essighaus" 1909. First, one had visited the Bremer Bleikeller to see old bog bodies under a huge Church. C. G. Jung reports how they had been almost fresh as life. "What do you see in these corpses!" the very excited Freud called out and promptly fainted. It was obvious to all that Freud had a "corpse in the cupboard". The scientific opinion of deep psychologists is that the "one killed" in this case was C. G. Jung, his rival upon whom he had subconsciously wished death or even Freud's brother Julius who had, without it having anything at all to do with Freud, died of tuberculosis in infancy.

Freud however was thought to have had a guilty conscience because he had wished "poisoned breast milk" upon his one-year-old brother. There is however no need for deep psychology to dig as milky-deep as that! After all, what is correct and important is so evident. Freud himself interprets his fainting episodes quite correctly: "The common reaction to a close friend or relative dying is to blame oneself for having played a part in causing that death" (Freud 1933, p. 553). Well: Freud killed neither Jung nor Julius. The corpse in the cellar emotionally close to him was called "Jahwe". And Jahwe will not be killed off entirely just like that. He remained just as fresh and hybrid in Freud's consciousness as a bog body. According to Freud, his fainting spells stood for the punishment of a murderer of God. What is more: From a point of view of religious psychology, Freud had been influenced by his nanny and was actually catholic. His father and mother had actually had almost no influence at all. His mother told Freud: "She carried you into all of the Churches; back home, you would preach and tell of what loving God does." Well, this God was not at all as loving as all that. After his visits to Church, little Sigmund was at the mercy of the most cruel of all of the approximately 5000 Gods known up to this day: Our Bible-God who threatens with a fire-hell nine times more than the much less dangerous Jahwe and finally drove Freud to feel so intensely guilty (Schur 1982, p. 235) that death was the outcome: Freud's " self-accusation", his fear of God's punishment according to the law of Talion resulted in an uncontrollable addiction to nicotine causing a carcinoma of the oral cavity. The Catholic Church therefore violently killed Freud with its threat of hell. As Freud thought God was a delusion, his subconscious had to consider him forever lost, for various Churches had taught him that only he who called to God shall be saved (Romans 10, 13, NT). Gods often have no sense of humor. His psychoanalysis was "a work of the devil" the Church called out to dying Freud in revenge. That makes him one of the many corpses in our so-called Christian Churches' cupboards. Dostojewski's fainting spells can be equally interpreted.

A classic translation of Freud's neurosis

Generally agreeing with the statement "Religion is insanity", all psychiatrists also develop a classic translation of Freud's neurosis. Like Freud, they believe in their subconscious that they have sinned by killing God. That is not true insanity! It is the consequence of an error we have been convinced of, a religious fallacy. Religion is no delusion but a religious fallacy. This lies in the presumption that God, who is love, might not like the idea of murdering his violent opponents Talmud-Jahwe and Bible-God who, to top it, are an invention of the clerics. Freud's sin was none and his fainting spells were just as unnecessary as Nietzsches schizophrenia. In four short meetings, I would have explained the interdependence and hopefully liberated him of his superfluous school notions – completely without using neuroleptics. When it was still common belief that the earth was flat, they were not all insane! They were simply mistaken.

To err was natural (and again typically human, typically clerical), it was obviously crazy that Galileo was to be burnt at the stake purely because he had contradicted the many religious dogma. Of course, nearly all baptized psychiatrists had virtually murdered God twice over. On the one hand, they are all supposed to be accomplices of Jesus' crucifixion, and on the other hand to be blamed for the death of his father by claiming that God was a delusion. This explains Peter Schellenbaum's question in "Gottesbilder", dtv, why deep psychology can only criticize Bible-Jesus in isolated cases: They feel they have sinned enough and may therefore sin no more. In this respect, "speaking medicine" remains silent or is and has sentenced itself to silence.

I herewith introduce the term "religious fallacy" into the psychiatric nomenclature as distinction to insanity. Attending a lecture on Freud will not turn anyone into an agnostic or an atheist – on the contrary, this is only achieved through hard work. With incredible naivety, in reality a safeguard mechanism, therapists postulate that children do not integrate the bible's fairy tales permanently in their subconscious, as they are too young, or then too old, to actually believe such nonsense. Therefore, according to them, the Churches do not induce disease, on the contrary, they are quite harmless and have up to date already "made great amends". No chance. This is all based on intellectual rationalization, spurred by the basic fear that criticism of the Churches is called for which represents a further act of sinning. All of my psychiatric patients critically mention the circumstance that their medical treatment does not include the religious issue. This catastrophe is caused not by evil intentions, but simply by an obsessional neurosis based on anxiety.

With his Theory of Sexuality and his neurosis, thought up as bulwark and dogma, Freud unintentionally leads psychiatry down a very dangerous cul de sac and up to the greatest professional negligence in mental health care, the ignorance of Church-induced disease. Caught up in Freudian neurosis, four times more psychiatrists than internists commit suicide, and for years psychiatry erroneously prescribed neuroleptics for diseases which could have easily been cured by talking. Freud's method of dream interpretation is more cumbersome, more time-consuming and far more prone to mistakes than EAT is. Hell as notion of a place actually awaiting us is so deeply entrenched in us that our subconscious only rarely allows us to appear in dreams. Wet-dreams however are far more frequent. As respects hated and demonized psychoanalysis, the measures of high-intelligence Church were as follows: It simply bought up. It bought the devil. Today, the majority of our psychiatrists is paid by the Church. And it will not tolerate any diagnosis criticizing the Church.

   The head of the institute examining me knew well of he works of Viktor E. Frankl, founder of logotherapy. Frankl virtually requires doctors to commit themselves to provide counseling, just as H. J. Weitbrecht, C. G. Jung, **Karl Jaspers**, Alphons Maeder, G. R. Heyer and others do (ref. Frankl „Ärztliche Seelsorge" in above-mentioned book, p. 67). Being baptized and ordained to mission as Lutheran priest, I have been committed virtually from the highest level (Christ's so-called Great Commission) to a mission that really allows God to impersonate Love and does not describe and therefore degrade him as the cruelest creature on earth in order to get financial self-interests. It illegally interferes with the practicing of my religion, if I am not allowed to preach the word of God, as it will have been understood by Jesus himself, in my doctor's practice. It is against Basic Law. Some colleagues of mine even pray with their patients. I, however, tend more towards trying to break the habit of excessive and disease-inducing praying, especially when it results in pathological, Church-intended humility.

Every therapist applying EAT (ecclesio-adverse therapy) (ref. my book "The Sacco-Syndrome") is a missionary in the sense that he must reduce a disease-inducing belief to absurdity. It is therefore a crucial part of our medical profession to mission in a super-religious sense or one that narrows the concept by representing a personal or anti-personal God who is purely – literally purely – unconditional love. Our profession must hold high ethical values such as compassion, love, justice, consideration and freedom and have the courage to tackle any cruelty in a religion immediately and urgently, even if the Church is the employer. Considering its diverse fault-finding ways, common religious practice up to now, however, is simply abusive – unfortunately often abusive of defenseless children. "What are we supposed to believe in if not in the bible?" clerics often ask me in despair. We are however not Christians in order to simply be believers but to work in the way Jesus had in mind for us and in doing so to fulfill his testament. Here Luther – as so often – was mistaken. After all, Luther erroneously thought it called for to set fire to Jew's living quarters thus making him the father of the Reichskristallnacht.

Having killed the Catholic God of Violence, he had been labeled a heretic and blasphemer.

The EAT

Now in EAT, the Ecclesio-Adverse-Therapy I developed, the therapist speaks openly about unlawful manipulation by the Churches, openly identifies correlations and in doing so lays the patient's subconscious at his or her feet so to say. That would not work with fear of castration because it does not represent the reason for the fundamental fear in the collective subconscious. Freud was unable to see the forest through the trees. Therefore, he considered a Bonsai tree to be the cause of anxiety instead of the devouring jungle, which I call the **Forest of Prometheus**. This forest corresponds with the "metaphysical mire" that Claire Goll writes about, and patients suffering from Church-induced disease often lead their therapists, who have not been educated respectively, deeply into this mire, leaving them no other way out than through depression or suicide. In this respect, it is crucial that they receive help.

Freudian theory has now been refuted. Time- and cost-intensive psychoanalysis will now have become superfluous in most cases. In the future, the therapist will be less silent and ask fewer questions, instead, there will be more answers and explanations. The great thing is, it works. A good EAT takes approximately four one hour sessions, followed a few short refreshments of what has been learned. Of course, a therapist must not enter this forest without being respectively qualified, i. e. not alone. He or she will get lost in and then possibly come down with similar subconscious feelings of religious guilt, like our hero in the Greek legend. Freud's subconscious knew why it had to switch off the doctor's conscious awareness now and then. EAT is also manageable for a layman on a smaller scale: Parents and grandparents can influence children to not believe everything the clerics or the evil bible says and not to hesitate to contradict when the most basic ethical values are being violated.

A religious reform

Meanwhile, what would be even cheaper than EAT would be a religious reform, and it is already certain that it is on its way. It was prescribed and introduced by the former President of our Federal Constitutional Court Prof. Papier with his groundbreaking words during his term of office saying that the Churches may have freedom of religious practice but have to stick to existing law. I herewith suggest nominating this expert in constitutional and public law for the Nobel Peace Prize. He provided the impetus for more long-term peace in the subconscious of our delinquents and seriously ill psychiatric patients. Freud's neurosis – also our psychiatrists' neurosis and unfortunately that of our society – has facilitated this innovation of our spiritual welfare. As if caught in Freudian loss of consciousness, it tolerates our Churches' incredible threats of torture not due to tolerance or even ignorance but from a real subconscious terror of God. The notion of death is so terrifying for children and adults that it can only be given a place in the subconscious. The fact that "modern" human beings view the holocaust Flood and Sodom and Gomorrah as just punishment and the penetrator of these crimes as some kind of honorable Mr. Clean.

Waiting time for appointments in the doctors' practices will then hopefully be reduced to a normal rate. Maybe even organized crime will be reduced and the therapy of offenders improved. Occupational therapy in our young offenders institutes will make no progress as long as the convicted persons are certain that the love of God is not meant for them, on the contrary: His much quoted wrath, a wrath and a brutality that do not exist, that, driven by financial self-interest, our Churches allocate to our God and his son. In doing so, the Churches label this alleged savage the greatest criminal ever and simply a non-Christian by making out that he has allegedly imposed punishment through fire on us. However, Jesus, who is one with God, is baptized! God is baptized!

I have taken a first step by filing three criminal complaints against our Churches depicting the child abuse they commit, and in doing so, I have shown a possible way to carry out the imminent reform. My Medical Chamber erroneously concluded that such a criminal complaint suggests that I might be insane, had not the prosecutor been lost for words upon hearing it! This authority had written to me saying that it did not agree with Prof. Papier's opinion. The Churches were allowed to break the law, they were allowed to threaten children with hell, blame them for Jesus' death and present the Holocaust to them as a just business, regardless whether or not it leads to serious diseases. All of this they consider "socially adequate". What is needed, therefore, are written statements to official bodies by persons who can affiliate themselves with my contrary opinion as well as with that of the German Federal Office for the Protection of the Constitution and to whom getting into trouble matters as little as it does to me.

" …we send to see … a theologian"

Patients with mental health issues must urgently insist on working through and learning to cope with the injuries they suffer due their religion in doctors' or psychiatric practices. This service is covered by the health insurance they pay for. Unfortunately, the professor M. Leuzinger-Bohleber who is considered Sigmund Freud's successor at the institute of the same name, states even in 2010 representative of our therapists: "Persons who have a theological problem we send to see … a theologian". Why? Because our thinking is not transcendental (quote from an interview in the newspaper "Die Zeit" of March 31, 2010). Sending away a patient like that is inappropriate for a doctor, as well as a lack of thinking in one's own specialty field. And, given that one is not thinking, is it not possible to at least start doing so?

So what is the outcome of such practices? The priest Johannes zu Eltz, loyal adherent of the Church and joining in the discussion, laments the considerable increase in the number of believers who fall seriously ill with schizophrenia due to the superstition they have been made to believe, or erroneous belief in hell and the devil respectively, which incidentally hardly a single psychiatrist distinguishes or is able to distinguish from true insanity. He will fall on deaf ears with the psychiatrist when he calls for "interdisciplinary work". Patients who are considered incurable for treatment from their psychiatrists would be sent to priests for further treatment. "No redemption without remorse", zu Eltz says in his characteristic fashion in a final interview and, in saying so, affiliates himself with his Church's very official doctrine that hell awaits those who do not do repentance or show remorse. In this respect he is wrong and proves the worst possible therapist of Church-induced diseases caused by fear of hell. These diseases should not be treated by those who caused them. Emotionally raped children should not be treated by the rapists.

"Possessed by the devil"

And is it surprising? Zu Eltz, who is not a doctor, misdiagnoses Freud's successor in a terrible and general way, leaving no room for doubt: The psychiatric, allegedly psychiatrically incurable, "insane" patients sent to see him were not paranoid psychotics but "possessed by the devil". An unbelievable scandal presents itself to us. Seriously ill patients whom we GP's have transferred to psychiatrists in good faith, are further transferred to theologians without our knowledge who then do not even write a report about what they are doing and inform us how they actually go about healing those who are possessed by the devil. Does one have them list all of their sins? Does one urge them there to confess and repent, given that they are already seriously ill with guilt? Does one even drive their obsession out of them using certain other measures?

Pope Benedict very successfully introduced and held well frequented crash courses in exorcism for priests. "The demonic penetrates all slots and cracks" is the title of the article in "Die Zeit" quoted here. This is what comes of increasing the amount of preaching about fear of hell. Incidentally, having knowledge (!) of the article, the psychiatrist judging me wrote that my mistrust of psychiatry was certainly paranoid. Her approach therefore bordered on crime.

We can go as far back as to Nietzsche who writes: "The worst thing that could have happened to Christianity is this type of preached "Christianity" of violence, and additionally a religion conveying such an intense fear of God that one feels obliged to help instead of simply behaving in a Christian manner and acting responsibly and motivated by understanding."

What shall we do?

What shall we do with our churches? Since 2008 the EKD (Evangelical Church in Germany) wraps itself in stony silence when I confront them with legitimate critical thinking. Silence on violence is but also violence that must be opposed. Leaving the church is one of the very efficient means of power to go against the power of the clergy and the nature of its violence. At the same time you can tell your church that you plan to reenter if they fulfill certain conditions. Accordingly I did so and also told the Hannover public prosecutor the following demands (excerpt):

"The provisional list of demands of the group 49 to my church is quickly assembled.
- Renunciation of ecclesiastical concept of hell as a threat
- Renunciation of the stories "Fall", "Flood", "Babylon", "Sodom and Gomorrah", where they are described as just judgments of God
- Add footnotes to the Bible to explain that as today's human beings we cannot identify ourselves with the text (for example: occurrence of a devil)
- Abolition of Eucharist as blame for the death of Jesus on the cross
- Deletion of John 8/44 and Luke 17 in the Bible
- Deletion of passages where God is described as the initiator of cruel punishments (examples: drowning, burning alive)
- New edition of hymnals with removal of all songs about hell and about the grace of God that should be necessary to escape this hell
- Prohibition of the Augsburg Confession
- Prohibition of the depiction of Jesus as a savior. Jesus has not to save us from anything.

We owe it to our mentally ill, especially the autistic, that the abolition of hell faith comes into play.

Of course you can achieve quite a lot with a suit. But I have the impression that the prosecutors feel an inclination to take their "colleagues" of the "public corporation" – the church – into custody. In this way they allow them to continue using the threat of hell as supposedly the best source of income.

They do this in the full knowledge that threat of torture is torture already and represents a strong prohibition. This of course also and especially for public corporations as are the churches. So it is indeed in our Constitution (dignity). Prosecutors often tell me that there are no proven victims. On the question of whether one is a victim of his church, the Sacco-Triad may help. Three things are required here: a mental illness, a feeling of being threatened by "God" (at least within the medical history of oneself) and an increased reflection on matters of belief.

The Cologne Regional Court clearly pointed out that religious circumcision is not allowed, since physical integrity is a basic right. The government now needs to quickly design a new law in order to convert such circumcisions into legality. This is the state of affairs 10/2012. But there will be no new law that allows the religion to continue the threat of eternal torture, because that would require an amendment of Article 1 of the "Grundgesetz".

But the lawsuit is a very effective way to draw attention to the fact that religious freedom has been widely restricted in this country for very good reasons. I just wonder: Why am I the only plaintiff. Because by being threatened with torture our core values and our children's health are obviously damaged – massively, daily.

Let us therefore finally wish for a psychiatry that is not afraid of the powerful but which finds the strength to question and doubt, that it can therefore change innovate things and can also gain independence from the of the organization Church which preaches violence.

According to Freud, however, the place of eternal damnation, the God who is supposed to manage that place and his devils happen to be pure delusions and therefore inventions of unscrupulous clerics who break the law by exercising terror. My patients share this opinion, and so do Schopenhauer, Rilke and some priests I know. Hell is not the notion of a God who loves us. In this good sense:

Take care, Yours Frank Sacco.

„Ihr seid nicht Schuld"

The poem

They say: They are criminals
I say: It's from fear
They say: It's cowardice
I say: It's from fear
They say: It's autism
I say: It is just from fear
They call their God the true love
I call him the God of Sodom,
the God of hell and fire
They say: It's religion
But it is just might and easy money
It's a business with that kind of fear
They say: "We give you great pleasure",
but they sing to a weeping God.

Contact / Imprint: Frank Sacco, internist, medical doctor, All rights reserved by the author.

Post Scriptum: If you, dear reader, feel as a patient at risk of any church or abused or harmed by psychiatry, or if you know cases where such is done, you are free to demand financial compensation or to make a complaint. It may not be your church. You can also as someone who is an atheist feel threatened, e.g. if you are told you would come into an eternal hell fire just because of your lack of church-membership or because you have not been baptized. If you complain, that is initially free (prosecutors, arbitration boards of the medical associations). Arguments for such an action are provided by this document. Your legal claims will also not become time-barred as churches constantly confront you with the threat of hell – officially and written in words, for example throughout the media. You only should be able to prove that this has happened.